Carving Pins

Mary Finn

Schiffer Publishing Ltd
4880 Lower Valley Road, Atglen, PA 19310 USA

Text written with and photography by Donna S. Baker

Dedication

To Stan, the love of my life, who always is there for me with his love and encouragement. For Carol Green, my best friend, who is a great source of strength, stability, and undying friendship, which helps make my life more complete and meaningful. Thanks for everything.

Copyright © 2002 by Mary Finn
Library of Congress Control Number: 2001097511

All rights reserved. No part of this work may be reproduced or used in any form or by any means—graphic, electronic, or mechanical, including photocopying or information storage and retrieval systems—without written permission from the copyright holder.

"Schiffer," "Schiffer Publishing Ltd. & Design," and the "Design of pen and ink well" are registered trademarks of Schiffer Publishing Ltd.

Designed by John P. Cheek
Cover design by Bruce M. Waters
Type set in Korinna BT

ISBN: 0-7643-1548-X
Printed in China

Published by Schiffer Publishing Ltd.
4880 Lower Valley Road
Atglen, PA 19310
Phone: (610) 593-1777; Fax: (610) 593-2002
E-mail: Schifferbk@aol.com
Please visit our web site catalog at
www.schifferbooks.com
We are always looking for people to write books on new and related subjects. If you have an idea for a book, please contact us at the above address.

This book may be purchased from the publisher.
Include $3.95 for shipping.
Please try your bookstore first.
You may write for a free catalog.

In Europe, Schiffer books are distributed by
Bushwood Books
6 Marksbury Avenue
Kew Gardens
Surrey TW9 4JF England
Phone: 44 (0) 20 8392 8585
Fax: 44 (0) 20 8392 9876
E-mail: Bushwd@aol.com
Free postage in the UK. Europe: air mail at cost.

Contents

Introduction

I love to give handmade presents for all types of occasions. A handmade gift is a gift from the heart – you give of yourself and of your talents. Depending on the occasion, it could be the present all by itself or given along with a purchased present.

Our family loves to camp and we spend much of the spring, summer, and fall enjoying this passion. Since you can't take a band saw with you to cut out blanks and space is limited, I had to come up with a fun and easy way to have gift projects available. Many of my students and other carvers have the same space problem, such as living in an apartment. Thus I came up with the idea of carving wooden pins. I can cut a number of the same or a variety of pins so I can quickly make a gift that will be enjoyed and used.

Start with an idea. Draw a basic picture of your idea but don't feel that you are stuck with it. Let your imagination go! You can get ideas from other pins you already have, greeting cards, rubber stamps, or computer graphics books (such as the one that catalogues your graphic library). Coloring books have simple drawings that often work out quite well and children's books are great for the same reason. Even the Internet can be a great source of ideas.

Once you decide what or who you want to carve, let your mind go – what characteristics or items do you associate with this object? Try to put these ideas onto paper either by listing or drawing your thoughts. I will often start with the basic outline then add the details.

Don't worry if you can't draw. You can use graphics, a copy machine, or a computer to do the drawing for you. The nice thing about using computers or copy machines is that you can size the project for the person you are making it for. You might want a smaller pin for your mother but a large "funky" pin for your younger sister. Dad might like a bolo using a medium size "pin" to form the interesting slide. Aunt Sue likes refrigerator magnets so size her project for keeping important notes on the fridge!

Once you have decided what you are going to make and have a picture of it, you need to determine if it will work. Is it too complex or too simple? What needs to be done to make it workable? For example, is the flower too busy and in need of simplification by having fewer petals? In other words, if you don't like what you see, make adjustments now before you mess up your pin or make an unworkable blank. Sometimes it is helpful if you leave the drawing for a while and come back to it after a period of time. Coming back with a "fresh" look can often solve any misgivings or problem areas.

Now you must get the wood and cut it out. Use a wood that will carve easily and keep the details, such as basswood. Hardwoods such as black walnut are great for flowers and should be left in their natural color to best show off the carving and the wood. Check around and see what you can find. Often, you can get scraps from other carvers. They may have pieces of leftover wood that is too small for their type of projects but would be perfect for pins. Also, try furniture makers, again asking for scraps. Take all offered wood then go home and select the pieces that will work. The remainder makes great campfire wood! If you have a good relationship with the person giving the scraps you could ask for only your favorite types of wood.

To cut out your blanks, draw, trace, stamp, or otherwise transfer the drawing to your wood. One neat trick is to get a copy machine or computer printout that is "fresh," then use an iron to "iron on" the picture to your wood. I like to use a glue stick to attach the picture to the wood. This allows me to really see what I want to do and have a better picture of what the finished project will look like.

Once your picture is on the wood you need to be able to cut it out. You can ask a friend for help but it is best if you can do it yourself. The best tool to use is a scroll saw, because it allows you to turn and go in any direction. Scroll saws are very safe and can be purchased fairly reasonably. Talk to other carvers to get their recommendations on specific models and maybe even get a chance to try their saw before purchasing your own. The only shortcoming of a scroll saw is that you can't cut thick wood, but since we are doing small projects, that won't be a problem.

Now it is time to get started...

Tools

Tools are very important to the carver. One's tools must be sharp and well maintained. Each carver has his or her own favorite tools – shown here are the ones I've used in this book. I consider them like a member of my family as I spend a lot of time with them! You do not have to have the exact same tool; something similar that you feel comfortable with will work.

First I have The Tool Family. Shown from left to right are a small skew, medium skew, large U-gouge, large V-tool, small V-tool, even smaller V-tool.

Next is the Knife Family, which includes the tools I probably use the most. On the left are two detail knives of slightly different shape; on the right are two X-Acto™ knives with different handles and blades.

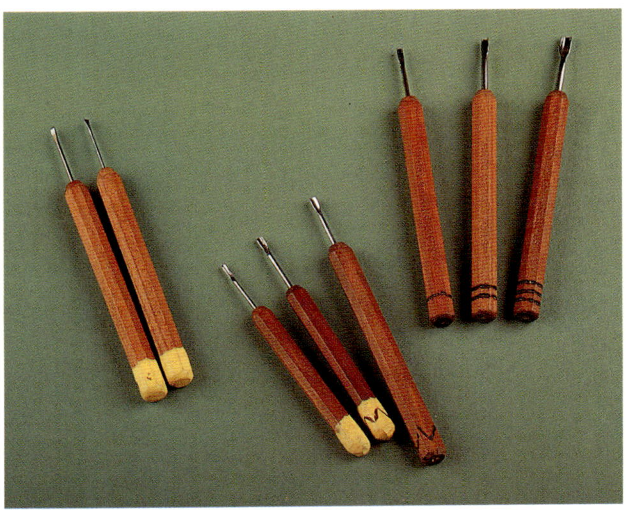

Last but by no means least I have The Micro Family, which I could not be without. Shown are skews, a variety of V-tools, and U-gouges.

The Sunflower

Before starting any of the pins, you need to come up with an idea, then design a blank, which is a precut piece of wood cut specifically for whatever you are going to carve. The blank will make it easier because most of the excess wood is removed. One type of blank can be created by using a foam stamp used for decorating, shown on the left. These come in a variety of shapes, sizes, and designs and are usually available in paint or craft stores. You can also draw your own design, like the one at bottom center, then trace it on your wood and cut it out. Another idea is to use a pre-made stamp or have a stamp made to your favorite pattern. This will allow you to make duplicates of the same pin very easily. The final outline, on the right, will be for the pin we'll carve first – the sunflower.

Here you can see again the outline I will start with to make the finished pin. I've drawn it on a piece of wood and will cut it out using a scroll or band saw. This piece of wood is 1/4" thick, so I would be cutting out a single pin. If I knew I wanted to make several of the same pin, I would use perhaps a 2" thick piece of wood, cut out the flower, then slice off individual pins to the correct thickness. Whenever you "slice off" individual pins from a thicker piece, use extreme care and holding devices and/or feeder-push sticks to protect fingers. The sunflower is a very simple pin to cut out, in that you go straight in, stop at the middle of the flower, very gently slide out, then come back in and meet the first cut. Slight curves may add more interest, but make it more challenging to remove the saw. A fine scroll saw would allow you to cut out the pattern in one continuous cut, twisting in and out as necessary. When drawing the outline for your blank, be aware of the wood's grain. Have it run so you get the most strength in the object you are doing. In this case, we'll have the grain running from left to right the long way across the flower.

Once the pin is cut out, start by drawing an oval for the center of the flower, then the individual petals. Note that I am using a marker to help you see the lines better; normally I use a pencil, as markers and pens tend to bleed and sink into the wood.

I am drawing in the individual petals. There will be one large complete petal, with a smaller, almost diamond-shaped area in between that petal and the next. As you draw the lines, try and give them an interesting rounded shape, to make your sunflower more interesting.

I've colored in the back petals on this blank so that as we continue on you will have no question about which are front petals and which are back petals.

V-tool the oval line to separate the center of the flower from the petals.

Now come back and stop cut in the deepest part of the V-cut. The reason we start with a V-cut is for the sake of accuracy: the knife is so sharp that if we tried to follow the original line we'd quickly get caught in the grain and possibly cut off a petal, or worse. The V-tool can make a number of small, very controlled cuts that can then form a track for our stop cuts.

Using your knife, taper the inner edge toward the flower's center. This will help to better define the middle of our flower from the petals. Don't worry about making the edge perfect – it's just a reference point for now. Your final shaping will come later.

Likewise, come back and slightly taper the outside of the V-cut towards the petals. Again, this helps improve identification of where the petals meet the center of your sunflower.

At this point, we need to establish the layers, or heights, of the petals. I'll do the back petals first, since they will be the lowest, or deepest, level in relationship to the other petals. To do this, first V-tool the outline of all the petals, then stop cut in the V-cut, then use a slice cut to lower the back petals. Be aware that each petal will carve differently because of the way the grain goes. Some will be very easy, some won't want to budge, others will want to pop right off. Be careful. In this picture I've done the first few back petals.

This is what your sunflower should look like when all the back petals are done. Notice that some of the petals are deeper than others. This adds variety and interest to the carving.

Next, round the center. This is accomplished by taking the edge of the original separation (shown by the red line) and bringing it toward the center. The area with the pencil line is further along so you can see where we're going. Continue towards the middle, as shown by the arrows. The center will still have a flattish look to it, but will now be rounded and somewhat "domed."

This is what your sunflower should look like when you have completed this step.

Now we can begin shaping the petals. I usually start in one place and work my way around, doing both the top and back petals as they come along. This way I know all the petals will fit together. Be sure and do the sides as well, creating a variety of shapes, levels, and flow to the petals. (Be aware that if you leave any of the original saw cuts, they will soak up the paint like a sponge when you begin painting.) During this shaping, I sometimes completely change the original cut-out shape of the petal, by shrinking it or thinning it out as desired.

All the petals have now been shaped and we are ready to paint. Our flower almost looks alive. Paint will really bring it to life!

Start by painting the whole flower a bright happy yellow. I prefer watercolors, because they allow more of the wood and grain to come through due to their transparent qualities. You could use acrylic paints, especially if they are watered down. I use the yellow in the center as well, even though the brown will cover it later. By painting the whole flower yellow I can be sure I won't leave any bare spots. Make sure the petals are well covered, though the center doesn't have to be as dark. Also, try to use a minimum of water as it raises the grain and will cause "fuzzies" on your finished flower.

Paint the center of the flower a warm brown. Try to vary the intensity so that your flower will look more natural.

I usually give the back side a coat of color and finish as well. This will protect it and give the project a finished look. Here I have used the same color as on the front. After painting, attach a pin by running a line of glue where you want the pin to be located. You can use super glue or a white glue. I'm using tacky glue here, which is a very sticky white glue similar to Elmer's but tackier.

I like to add "freckles" to my sunflower for more interest and reality. The center of a real sunflower is very detailed, but freckles will work well here. Be sure your freckles are very random and haphazard.

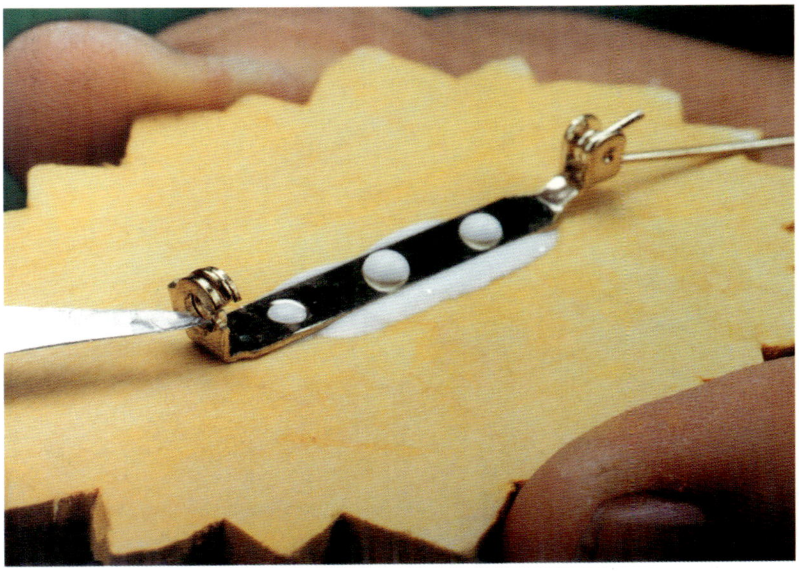

Below: To complete the sunflower pin, we need to seal and finish it. I use a water based acrylic varnish, easily available at hobby and craft stores. Here I have applied the finish only to the petals so you can see the difference in shine. If you prefer the center flat, you can use a flat finish. Don't leave any area without a finish, as it will be open to dirt and moisture.

Above: When you place the pin on the glue, make sure the glue bubbles up through the holes, forming a round bead. This helps keep it securely attached to the wood. Notice where my knife is pointing. This is the opening where the pin fits into the lock. Make sure you position the pin so that this opening is facing what will be the bottom of the pin. If your pin should happen to unclasp, it will then be less likely to fall off and get lost.

The Cardinal

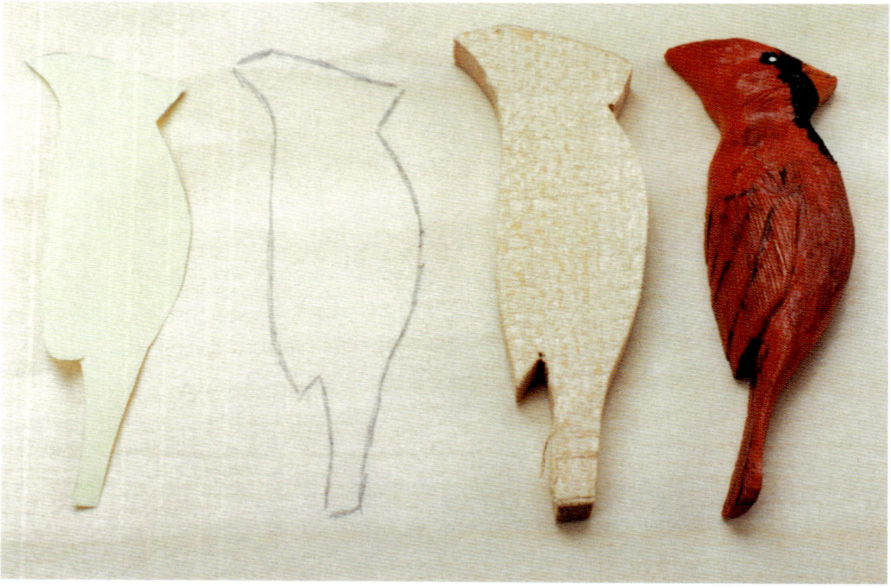

We start first with a template, in this case a small piece of paper. As you can see, I traced the outline from the paper template onto my piece of wood and then cut it out. Note: the grain of the wood should go up and down the cardinal from head to tail. This gives strength to your project. At the far right you can see what the finished cardinal will look like.

Next draw some basic lines on your bird. I usually start with the wing line, using the indentation between the tail and the tip of the wing to help me know exactly where the wing line should be. Now draw the beak – it is also easy to locate and serves as a landmark on the bird. Notice that for both of these I drew a thick solid line. For illustration purposes, I have again used the marker. Normally I would use pencil so I won't have to worry about erasing the lines later or having them bleed on me. I have also put in a dotted line (I even added red so you could see it better) to suggest where the high point of the bird's cheek might be. This line is dotted to remind me that it is a reference line only – it will be neither V-cut nor stop cut.

Now V-cut the wing line, then come back and use a stop cut in the deepest part of the v.

To further define and separate the wing from the body, slice from under the wing up towards the wing. Continue the whole length of the wing, further separating the wing from the body.

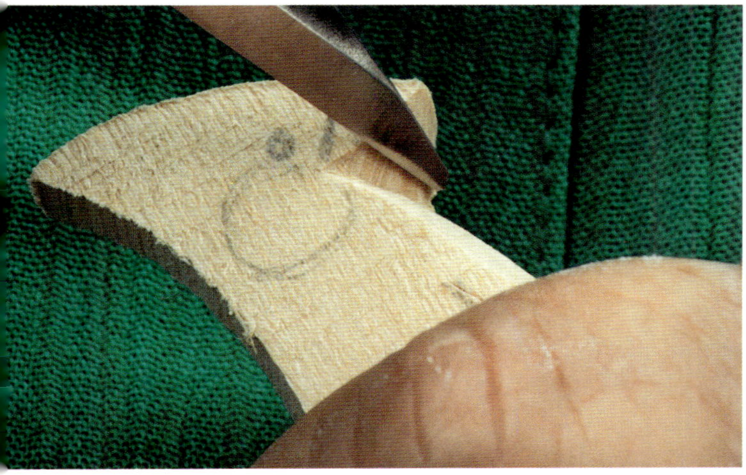

Next, V-tool and then stop cut the beak lines. Now slice down on the bottom half of the beak, making it look triangular.

Start rounding the body by removing the hard, straight edge all the way down the front side of the bird.

Now shape the upper half of the beak, blending that back to the bird's "pompadour." Note that this part is angled from the tip of the beak to the tip of the pompadour and also from the approximate eye area down to the edge, giving the upper head a rounded shape toward the edge.

Remove the hard edge along the outside edge of your pin. Basically, we are taking a little bit all over, knowing that more detailed shaping will come later for a perfect cardinal or "birdie" shape.

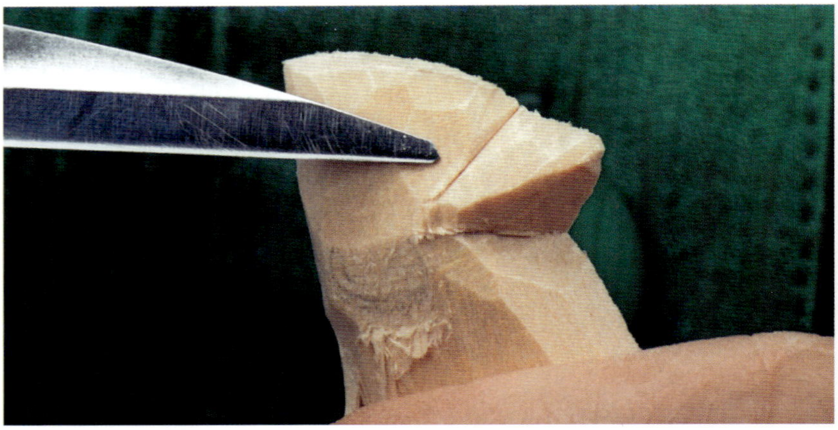

To separate the beak a little from the face, let's go over our stop cut and taper the beak under this cut, since the beak edge is covered by feathers on a real bird.

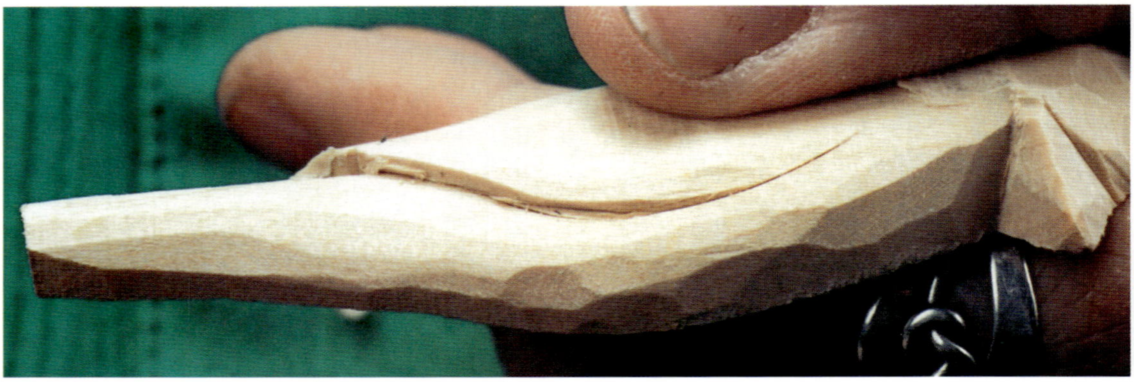

I have now increased the height of the separation between the bird's body and the wing and have also rounded the body all the way to the bottom of the tail. It's not completely finished up by the head, however. I left some extra wood there so I could shape the cheeks and create an indentation between the body and the head.

Round the wing to the outside edge and down towards the tip, as indicated by the penciled arrow. This is done to suggest that a wing is thicker at shoulder level, tapering to the tip.

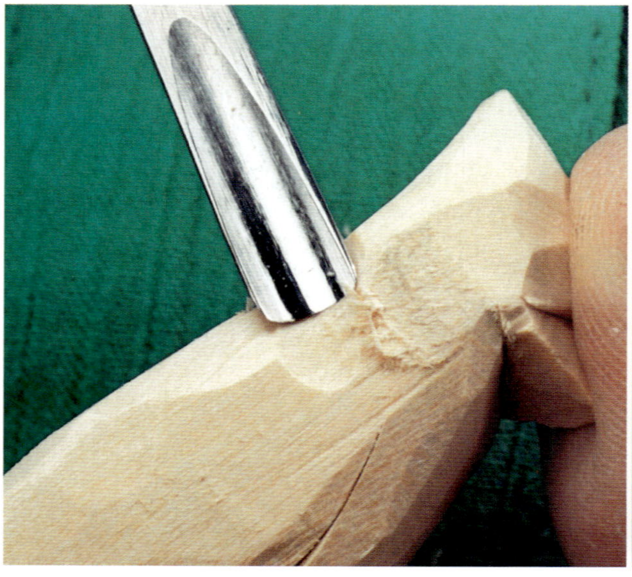

Make an indentation for the shoulders and the separation between the head and the body. I start by using a U-gouge, coming around under the cheek and the beak. Notice on the completed bird how there is an indentation for the eyes, then the puffy cheeks, and then a wider, broader arch that forms the separation between the head and the body. The arch is what I'm working on in this step.

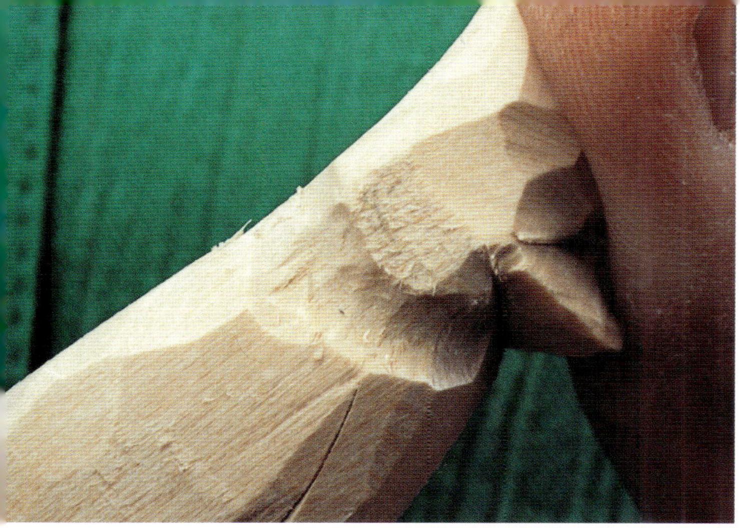

Here's what you are aiming for at the completion of this step: a well defined separation.

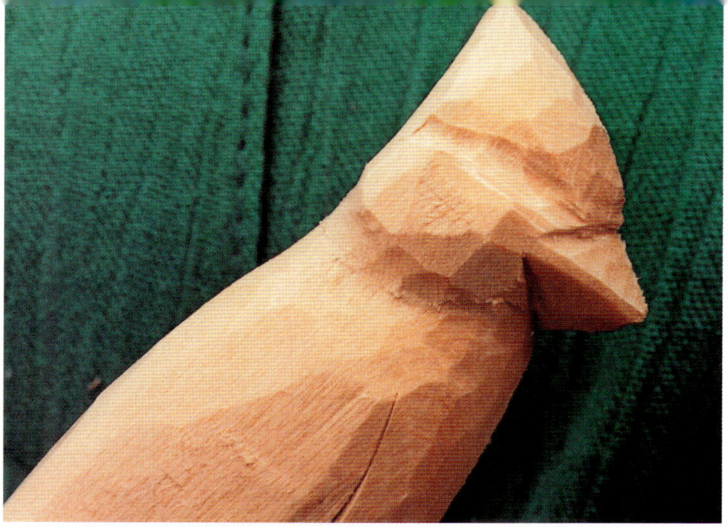

Round the cheek and, if you need to, take down the beak a little to get a nice fit and shape all the way around.

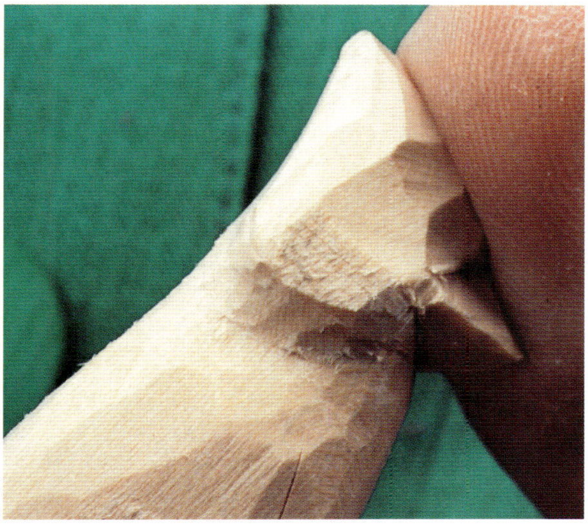

Feather the edges of the U-gouge for a nice blended line. Also smooth out the indentation itself up to the cheek, but not onto it. You are fighting the grain here a little bit so take your time and take many small cuts. Try not to leave a line of demarcation – we want a nice smooth flow. Sometimes coming back with a smaller U-gouge to knock off the "heads" of the unreasonable pieces is helpful. Here it is close to done, but you'd want to continue till it was really nice and smooth.

I needed to thin out the pompadour as it was sticking up way too high and needed to have a more pointy appearance. I will also correct any rounding problems (perhaps even thinning the tail), then I'll be ready to draw on some feather lines. I try to suggest a natural bird wing with smaller rounded feathers at the top and long "flying" feathers underneath. I've also drawn a small circle where the eye will later be painted on.

Let's start making the indentation for the eye. It will help further shape the cheek and head, giving us a place to locate the actual eye.

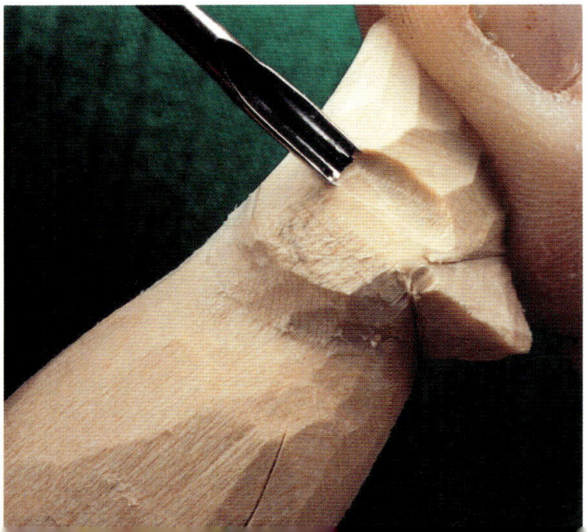

V-tool the feather lines, using a very fine V-tool and a light hand. You should even have to erase some of your pencil line if you've done it correctly. Here I've done the bottom two longer lines only. Now stop cut the V-cuts, then gently taper the bottom feather under each upper feather.

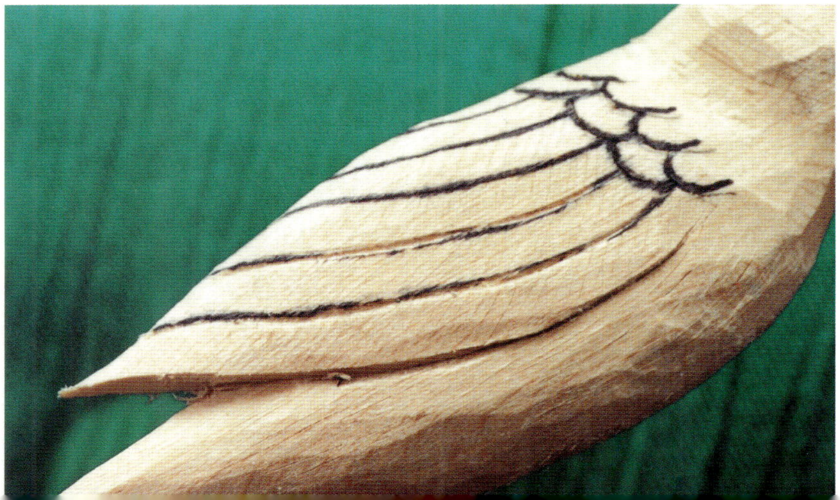

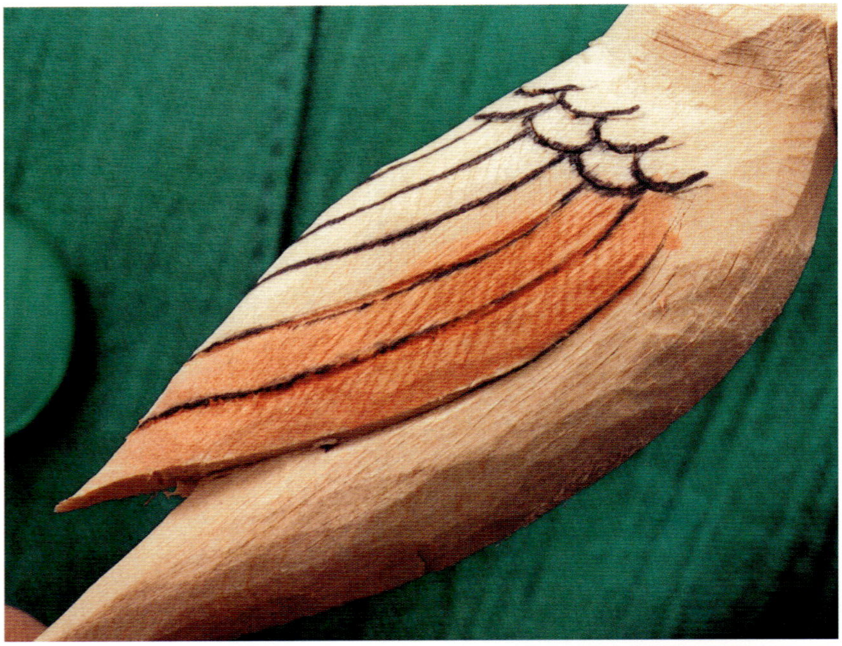

Take a very fine bladed knife (such as an X-Acto™ knife) and make very, very fine lines on each feather down to the edge of the next, giving the cut a slight arc. You can barely see them until they have a little paint on – then miraculously they appear. This is a small bird, so you don't want very fat lines. A fine woodburner would also work for this step.

Texturing is a very important part of making our bird look more realistic, as you can see on this completed model. Starting with the head, I made fine cuts to suggest the feathers. They start at the beak and go to the tip of the pompadour, then follow along the cheek and down to the neck. After completing the remainder of the feathers on the wing, I added texture to the torso area as well. This bird has a nice wide tail, so I used individual lines to suggest feathers then added texturing similar to the wing.

Since this is a rather simple paint job, I won't illustrate each step but will describe the process. First paint the cardinal red all over – use a vibrant red to match the natural colors. After the red dries, paint the beak orange, then add the bird's signature black mouth and upper breast area. Use soft gentle edges, rather than straight lines – after all, we are talking about feathers here. For the eyeball, paint on a simple black circle with just the tiniest dot of white for a highlight. You can also draw a line for the separation of the beak. If you are not comfortable using your paintbrush, substitute a permanent, extra fine marker. As with the sunflower, I have used watercolors so that the lines carved for detailing show through better. To emphasize the feathers and bring out all the highs and lows, you can also make a very watered down black wash and use it to quickly, lightly coat the wing, breast, and tail area. Apply the finish, then when dry add a pin to the back the same as we did with the sunflower. Enjoy!

The Bunny

As with the previous two pins, begin with a template. Draw the outline on a piece of wood and cut it out with your saw of choice. The grain should be running from the tip of the bunny's ears down through his mouth, to prevent you from having a delicate part lopping off at the most inopportune moment. This is what you will end up with.

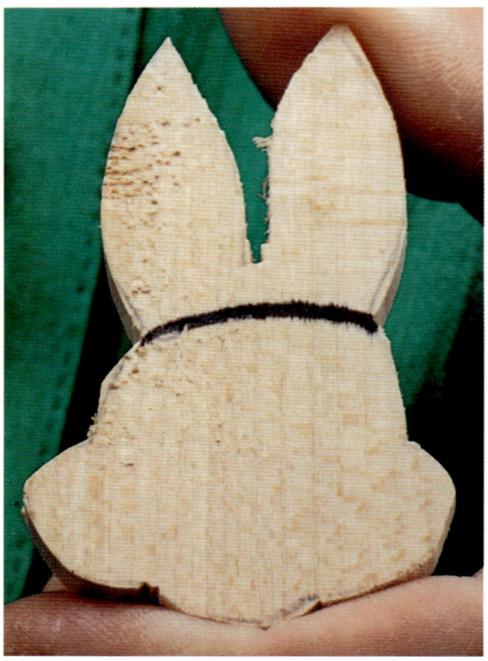

Draw an arc at the top of the bunny's head. Depending on your blank, it might or might not reach the opening between the ears. Here I have intentionally made mine so it doesn't touch, to let you see that this is OK. During the carving you will correct this.

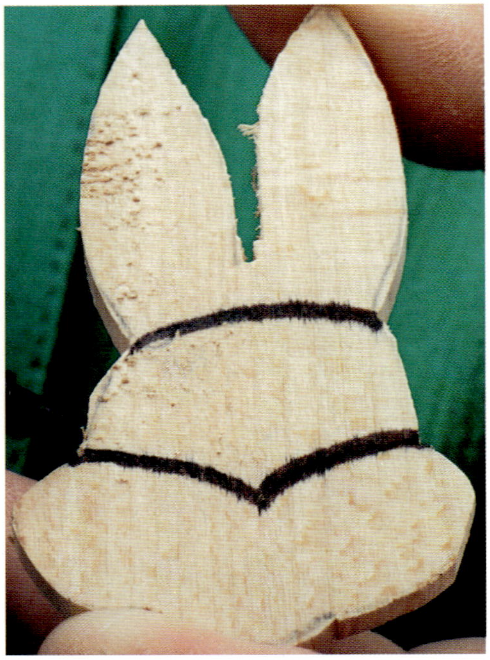

Next draw a graceful arc from the outside edges where the cheeks will be, coming to a point in the middle of the blank where the nose will be.

Draw the nose by simply making an arc over the point of the line you drew in the previous step. Then, following the contour of that same cheek line, draw two circles or ovals to form the bunny's whisker mounds.

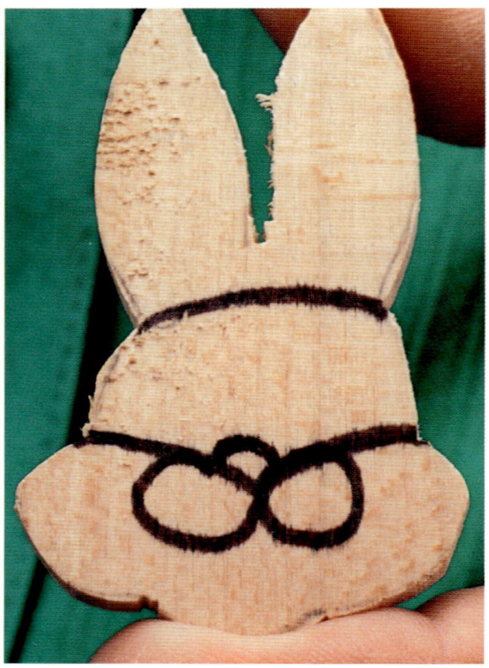

Since we're in this area, let's go ahead and draw in the mouth and teeth. I like to make the bunny look real cute and happy.

Add the eyes next. Draw a large "arched" area for the outside edge of the eye. Then color in the pupil, which is quite large. I have also completed the center ear line.

Lastly, draw in the openings for the ears. Now we have a completed drawn blank ready for carving.

Continue lowering the ear surface so that you end up with a nice flat surface with a significant height difference between the ears and the rest of the blank. No shaping is done at this point; we are only establishing heights or levels.

V-tool all the lines, with the exception of the inside of the ears. We'll do those later with a U-gouge to get a more rounded, softer edge. Don't stop cut at this point – we will stop cut each area as we go along. We V-tooled all lines to prevent losing any parts of the bunny as we carve.

Now stop cut the cheek outline and the nose, then lower the face so that it is a slight step below the cheek/nose level. The cheek/nose will be the highest area of the pin.

Stop cut in the line that you made for the top of the head, then slice towards that line to lower the ears, as they come from the middle of the head, not the edge.

When you are done, the rabbit should look something like this. Again, you want a flattish plane, not shaped yet. The height difference is less than that of the ears to the head. Note that this lowering of the face has cut in half the difference between the ears and the face. That's why the ears were originally lowered so much.

Stop cut around the whisker mounds and lower the remainder of the face, again using small slice cuts. You don't want much of a difference, just enough to slightly round the whiskers.

Your bunny's face should now look something like this. Notice that there is very little difference between the height of the whisker mounds and nose versus that of the lower portion of the face.

I'm starting to round the upper portion of the face. I begin by tapering the edges of the head more under the cheeks. I will then continue around the whole face, getting rid of the sharp edges and rounding towards the middle and the edges.

This is where you should be now. Notice that the center is still somewhat flat, to leave a nice space for our eyes. But you should start to see the bunny ready to burst out.

Now on to the cheeks. We will start by rounding the edges. Notice that I have drawn a dotted red line as a reference point to show where the cheeks will round towards the mouth. I'll actually make a small indentation here. In this photo, I've carved on the left side only to better show the difference. Note that this area still needs more overall rounding. I like to get the pin "in the ball park" so that I know everything fits before perfecting any one part!

Be sure to go all the way down to the edges. Short, small cuts are the best way to achieve accuracy in this rounding process. After you complete the rounding of the cheeks they should look like this – again, to highlight the difference, I have rounded only the left side on this bunny. You can see by comparing the two sides how much wood I have removed. My knife is pointing to the place where the cheeks, whisker mounds, and face come together. I have made what I call a "magic triangle" here, coloring it in with pencil so you can see it better. I like to call this a "magic triangle" because it does so much to further enhance the rounded look of the cheek. After removing this magic triangle, the face really becomes more natural looking.

Next we will shape the mouth mound. It will be highest in the middle, tapering to either side, and nicely rounded. Here I have shaped and slightly lowered the side to the left of the dotted black line, leaving the other side alone for illustration.

Here's what your bunny should look like at this point. Sometimes I'll go back and adjust the top of the head if I think it needs a few extra cuts here and there to make everything fit together nicely. You can see that I've redrawn the teeth and the mouth line to help you better visualize the finished pin.

Ears are next. First redraw the inside of the ears, if needed. Then start with a U-gouge, placing the tool so the outside edge of the gouge lines up with the line. The size of the gouge is not that important – you just want to start digging down (but not through!) at this point.

Dig down to the desired depth. Use a stop cut where the U-gouge meets the head to get rid of any extra ear particles. To smooth the ear, come back with a larger U-gouge, which will remove the ridges of the smaller U (it's much safer starting with the smaller gouge so you don't take out too much at a time). You can see on the upper ear how smooth it has become with the larger gouge. The lower ear shows what it looks like after using the smaller gouge only, prior to the smoothing process.

Even though the area closest to the point of the ear is smaller than this large gouge, by turning the tool on its side no area is unreachable.

We are now ready to begin shaping the whisker mounds. To start rounding, carefully remove the edges first, slightly tipping the whisker mounds under the nose and towards one another. Here I have done only the left side so you can see the difference. Make any adjustments to the cheek as needed. Also be sure to remove all the saw lines.

When you have completed both whisker mounds, the bunny should look like this. Note that I used a very thin blade, enabling me to take off very small pieces of wood, almost like giving our bunny a shave.

The nose needs just a minimal amount of shaping. Take off the edges, but keep the nose fairly high. This is a very delicate piece and if you are not careful you could lose the whole thing. Small cuts will work best.

Redraw the eyes and the lines of the mouth. Be sure to use pencil so your lines don't become a permanent part of the finished pin.

Now V-tool the outside line of the eyes, using a very soft and gentle touch and a number of individual cuts so you don't go running off your intended objective. Your tool needs to be very sharp for this step. Next, stop cut in the line and taper the inside of the eye very slightly towards this line, using a very sharp knife. In this picture, both eyes have been V-tooled, and the left eye has also been tapered. The tapering will become much more evident once the bunny is painted. Note that the blackened, colored in dot will be painted rather than carved.

On to the teeth and the mouth. First V-tool both lines, being very careful to make a number of smaller cuts rather than trying to do it all at one time. If you get caught in the grain, try turning the bunny around and coming at it from a different direction.

Using a very small U-gouge, lower the area inside the mouth between the teeth and the lip (the two lines that you just V-cut). Again, work slowly so you don't lose the teeth.

A denture brush can help greatly in cleaning out this area (or any other area with fine, little loose "chips").

Come back with your sharp knife and make straight edges on the teeth – this will help to further shape up this area. Clean up outside the U-gouged area as well to make a nice smooth surface where the lip will go. Here I am using a skew to flatten any bumps or undesirable spots on the inside of the mouth.

U-gouge around the outside of the opening to form the bunny's lip. A number of small cuts is again recommended. It doesn't have to be extremely high, just enough to suggest a lip.

Now blend the bottom of the U into the chin for a smooth appearance with only the lip raised. I've drawn a line right by where I'm smoothing to make this clearer for you.

The final touch for the mouth is to be sure the teeth are nicely clean and flat. Use either your knife or V-tool to make the separation, depending on the size of the teeth. I used my knife on this one, as I was afraid my V-tool would split this small, fragile area.

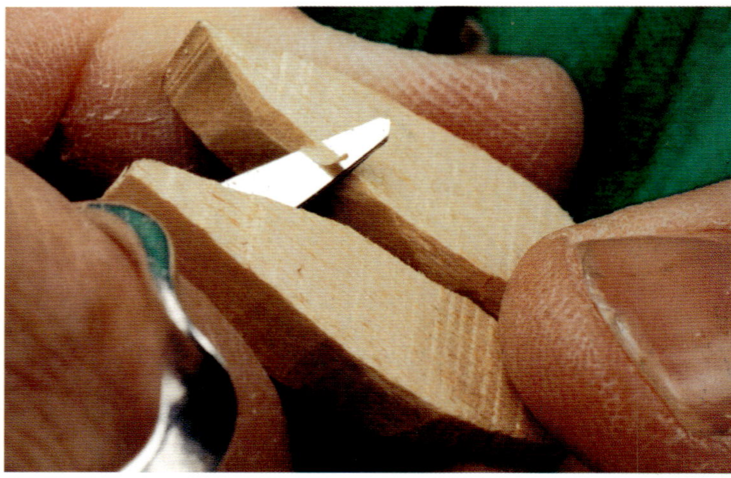

Go over your bunny to be sure all side edges have been finished and no loose particles are hanging around. As shown here, I sometimes take a little off the back of the ears to give them a neater, more rounded look.

The bunny is ready for painting.

Be sure the white paint is completely dry before moving on to the next step. Then mix some white acrylic with a red water-color to make a nice soft pink for the inside of the ears. Use this same pink for inside the bunny's mouth. Add a bit more red to get a brighter color for the lips. Before you go any further, put on a light coat of water based varnish. I do this before painting the eyes and nose, because the varnish can cause the paint to run. If the eyes and nose were already done, they could bleed into the face when I put on the varnish. Be sure to get the varnish on all your edges before adding any details.

Now I have painted in the outline of the eye, using either a paintbrush or a very fine black permanent marker. Then I added the colored part of the eye, followed by the nose, and a few strategically placed dots on the whisker mounds.

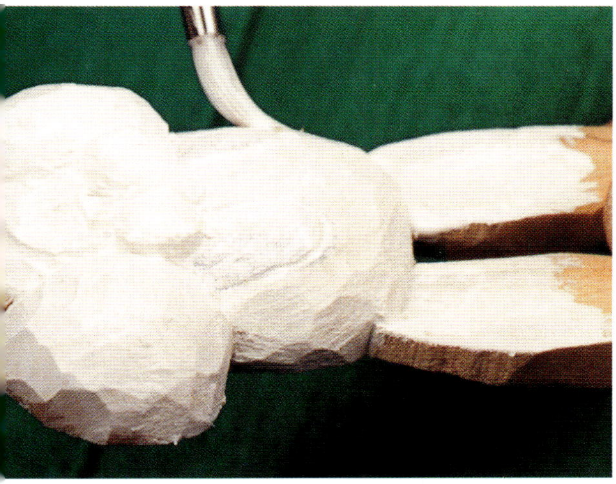

Left: Start the painting by using white over the entire bunny. I'm using a slightly watered down acrylic here. I usually prefer watercolors, but the white in a watercolor tends to be too faint. Be sure you get into every single crack and crevice. Also, don't have your paint too watery or you will raise the grain again. If that occurs, you will need to tidy up and then repaint that area.

Right: I like to paint the back as well, to give it a completed, finished look. I do more of a wash so that the wood shows through. The back can be painted in one of the colors from the front or any other color you like. The advantage of using the main color from the front is that if it bleeds over you won't notice it. I'm going to turn this pin into a magnet, by using a self stick strip of magnet. Just peel off the protective paper and attach the magnet to the back. Use a little glue in addition if necessary. Another option would be to make the bunny into a tie tack, a bolo, or anything else your imagination comes up with. Let your imagination go wild!

The Santa

As with the previous pins, start by making a template of your project – drawing it on your wood then cutting it out. Next, draw the appropriate lines to provide an outline of your intended carving. For Santa, I like to draw the hat first, starting with the ball, because its location will be obvious. Then draw the brim, giving it shape and a little roundness. Next add a line for the tassel. Draw the nose in next. It doesn't have to be very detailed – I have drawn just a basic outline here. Follow that with the rounded cheeklines and some eyes, created with two simple dots and lines above them. Finish with a mustache and some lips. You are not "stuck" with this drawing – it's just to give you an idea of where all the parts will go.

Let's begin with the hat. Stop cut the lower line of the hat where it comes in contact with the face. Then lower the face under the hat.

When teaching these steps, I often have a number of Santas ready to show each part of the process. This allows my students to progress at their own rates. On our Santa, I have V-cut all the lines with the exception of the eyes and the nose. This will help to prevent losing any lines during carving, as well as letting us see how different options will look.

Next, stop cut the upper line of the hat brim and the tassel line. Lower the hat area so that the brim is the highest part of the hat.

Lower one end of the brim slightly so that the tassel appears to be on top of the brim. Also remove a triangular area on the hat so that the tassel will appear higher than the hat and the brim, but the hat will still be lower than the brim. I've colored in this area for greater clarity.

Stop cut the line at the bottom of the nose. Note that this line has never been V-tooled.

Next we need to lower the tassel under the ball. I'm pointing to the area that I've lowered and have also colored it in so you can see it better.

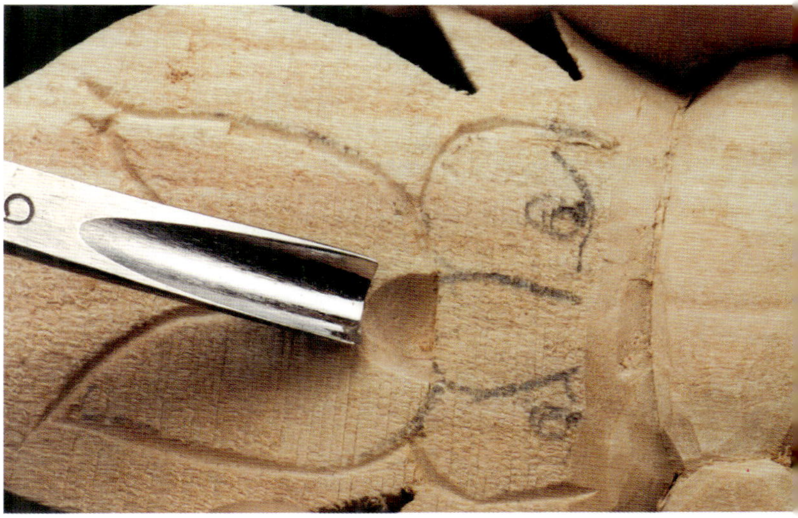

Now U-gouge up to this line, so that the nose will start to stick out from the face.

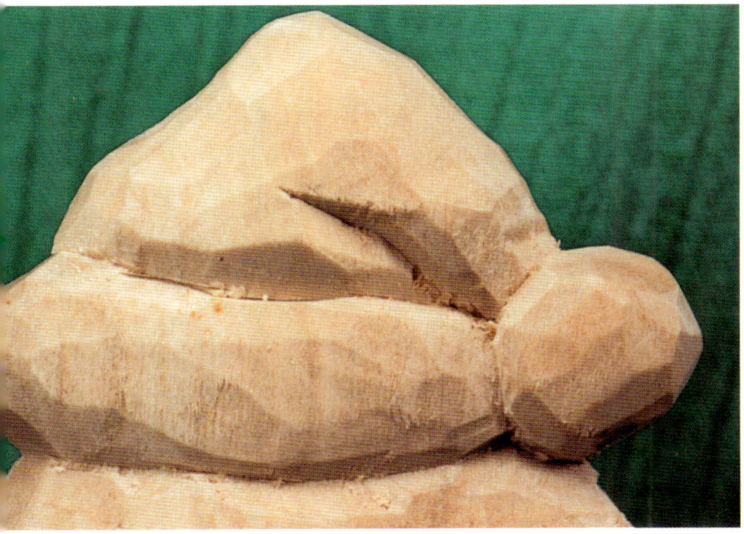

Round and shape the hat, referring to this photo for help with shaping. Remember to always start with the edges and work towards the middle.

U-gouge up the sides of the nose. This will start the shaping of the nose as well as separating the nose from the face.

Angle slice up to the top of the nose. The nose should be wide at the bottom, slender at the top. These cuts start to make the nose more triangular in appearance. Come back and repeat as needed for better shaping.

The nose should look like this when you have completed the previous step. It doesn't have to be very clean at this point – after we put in the eye socket we'll be able to go back and tidy things up.

Next are the eye sockets. Make a slice from the top of the eye down to the approximate middle of the eye. It doesn't have to be really deep, but must be lower than the nose as it tapers back from the top.

Now come back and form an angle from the underside of the eye. Because we are working on a flat surface, the eye socket will be slightly uphill towards the hair. Here you can see both eyes with the socket already begun. I am also starting to taper the cheeks up towards the eye sockets.

Next I will stop cut in the V outline of the face, since we need to further shape the eye socket as well as the face.

Tuck the edges of the face under the hair. This will allow more room to get in and correct that uphill slant of the eye. The side with my knife has begun the tapering, while the other side is simply at the stop cut stage.

Here I am making the eye socket more level and giving a little more shape to the cheek.

Let's give some attention to the nose. With a U-gouge, go straight in approximately one third up from the bottom of the nose. This will help to create the rounded part at the bottom of the nose. I like to call these the orbs.

Now taper the extra wood left by the U-gouge cut so that the nose becomes more triangular and shapely. We don't want Santa to have an ugly nose!

Let's turn Santa right side up so you can see where we're at. Notice that I've only been working on the left side for comparison purposes.

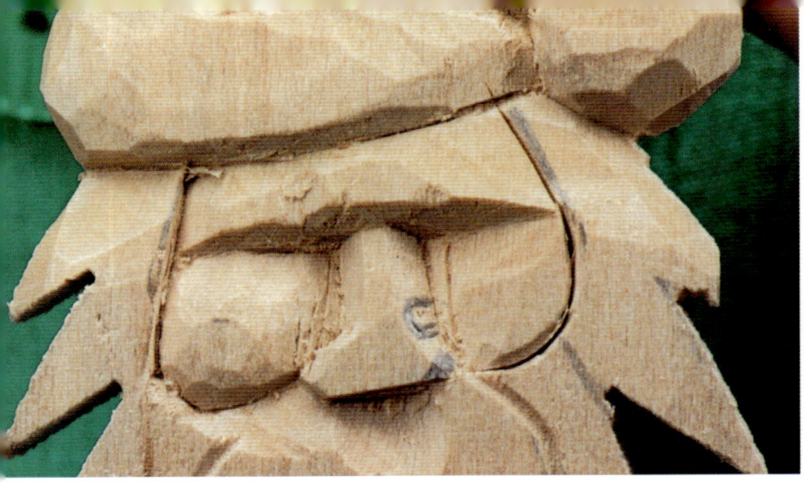

Tuck a little of the cheek and mustache under the nose and remove a small triangle from the corner of the nose to give the nose a more rounded appearance. This is another of what I refer to as "magic triangle." It is such a little thing but does so much. I've colored this triangle in on the right so you can see what I removed on the left. I've also drawn a little sideways U to show you where I used my U-gouge way back at the beginning of the shaping.

Here's how your Santa should look when you've completed the above steps on both sides. On this Santa I've also taken my U-gouge and made a cut to give more shape to the forehead. I made this cut by starting at the brow, gouging up to the hat. It is a shallow cut. Doing this gives a more rounded and natural appearance to the forehead and eyebrow area.

You can begin shaping Santa's hair now. It basically just goes up towards the head. You can exaggerate the separation between the two tufts of hair on either side if you want, even adding a curled look if desired.

Don't forget to carve the undersides of the cheeks. Also, make sure you have a distinct separation between the beard and the hair.

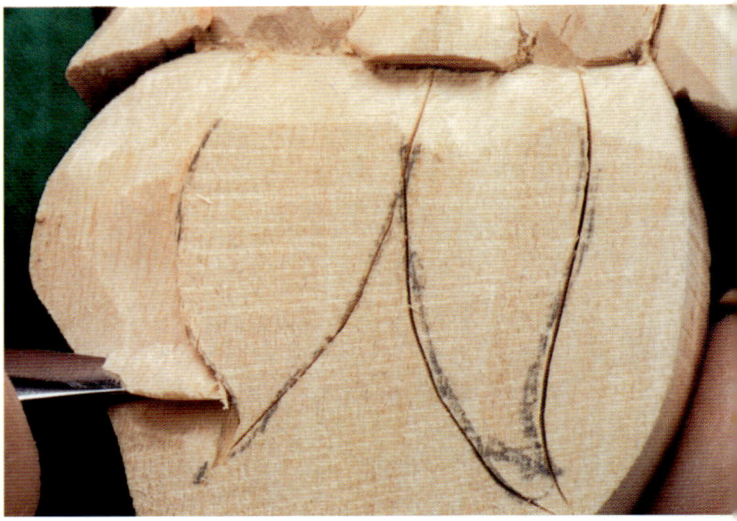

V-tool the lines of Santa's mustache. Stop cut in your V-cut lines and then lower the area on either side of the mustache.

Now that you have lowered the mustache from the beard, go ahead and round both the mustache and the beard, adding curves and curls to make them more interesting. Start at the edges and move in towards the middle. Here's what you are aiming for.

Draw on the eyes. I've gone ahead and put in two eyes, but the side with the pencil pointing to it is much larger than the other side, since the area for the eyes was different. This does happen, but don't worry – it's fixable! Simply remove some wood off the outside edge of the eye on the hair side, tucking and shaping until the eye sockets are more equal and pleasing.

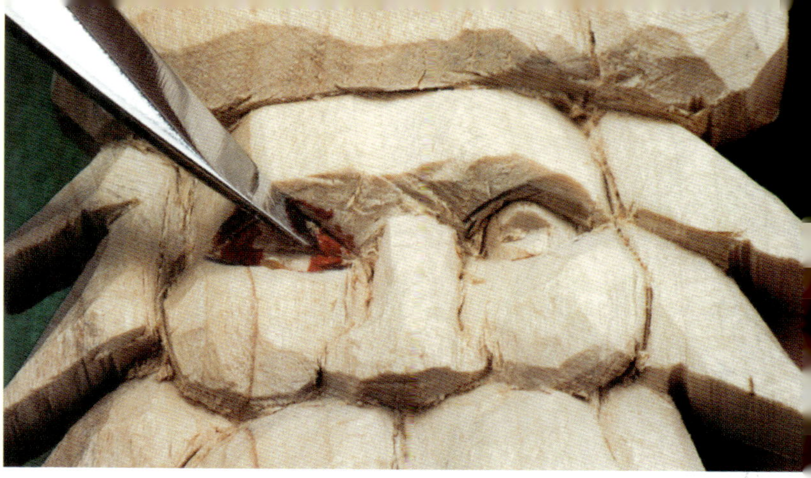

Stop cut in the V-cut line you just made, then come back and remove a magic triangle in both corners of each eye. I've colored the triangles in red on the left. Note that the angle of my knife is the desired angle. You want to be deepest in the corner of the eyes so that it will taper towards the middle of the eye. This will help with the rounding process. The eye on the right shows what it should look like.

I will make a little scooped out area by the corner of both eyes since a head has a natural indentation near the eyes. This will further adjust our uneven eyes. Here I used red so you could compare the old eye with the new.

Tuck and shape both eyes for a pleasing, rounded look. If some of the crease in the center of the eye from the eye socket remains, don't worry – this won't show up once your Santa is painted. In fact, I'm pointing to a little of the crease that I've purposely left here, to prove my point. Keep in mind that if your eye looks too sunken from the cheeks or upper part of the eyelid, you can lower the edges of the eye until it tapers smoothly with the cheeks or upper eyelid.

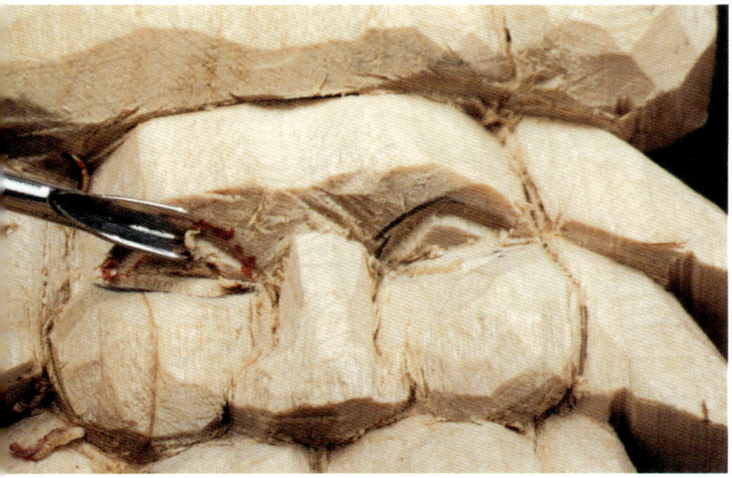

Starting in the middle of each eye's arc, V-tool towards the corners. Go back to the middle and do the other side, then repeat on the bottom line.

Now I am going to add some bags under Santa's eyes for character and expression. I use a simple V-tool to make two lines, starting from the middle of the eye and going up towards the point of the nose. The line closest to the eye should be a bit longer than the line furthest from the eye.

This Santa is going to get some wild eyebrows. I've drawn them on to start. Notice that I used a lot of small points, which will make the lowering process easier.

V-cut and then stop cut the eyebrows, then lower the area around them slightly so the eyebrows stand out. Don't be overly concerned if you can't reach into certain areas. The painting will bring out the eyebrow for you. I'm pointing to the area that is most important to lower.

To make the nostrils, so our poor Santa can breathe, simply take a U-gouge and go straight down at the bottom of the nose. Add any extra roundness that is necessary. On this Santa, the mustache is rather close together and covering the mouth. If I put a mouth in now it would be so far down into the beard that it would look odd. If you had a more open mustache and wanted to add a mouth, however, you would start by making an opening for the mouth, then come back with a U-gouge to form the bottom lip. The technique would be similar to that used on our bunny project.

The last part of the carving is Santa's hair, which includes the mustache, beard, hair, and eyebrows. In order to make hair realistic and interesting, I start with the larger V-tool and make a variety of flowing cuts – some long, some short, some in the middle. The three on the right that I've put a pencil line in will give you an idea of how these should look. I then come back with the small V-tool to fill in the blanks and add interest. Do this for all the hair on your Santa.

Santa is now ready for painting and finishing. Start by painting the flesh of the face. Paint all over, even inside the eyes. Then add the white, making sure that the flesh has dried thoroughly. White is used for the beard and hair, the brim of the hat, and the ball at the end of the tassel. I also use white to color the inside of the eye and, carefully, the eyebrows. If I need to take a little license with the eyebrows, I can do so. In fact, they can be all painted in rather than carved, if desired. Next I paint the hat red. Lastly, I've given this Santa green eyes with a little white for the twinkle in his eye. Finish with a coat of water based varnish. At this point I can add my pinback or magnet, or use Santa for another purpose if desired.

The Rose

For this project I like to use a paper pattern, which lends itself to peeling off in stages as the petals of the rose are carved. To make this one, I originally drew the pattern, then scanned it into my computer. This lets me print it out whenever needed. You could also use a rubber stamp to print the pattern onto paper. Using a glue stick, I then glued the paper pattern onto my piece of wood, with the grain going up and down through the rose, and cut it out with a saw. In this case, I am using black walnut, as rather than paint it I am going to use the beautiful texture and color of the wood as is. To begin your carving, V-tool all the lines. Take your time, making a lot of small cuts, as there are a lot of angles here. Don't be upset if the paper pattern tears a bit.

Once all the lines have been V-tooled, stop cut the leaf at the bottom left. I start with the leaves as they are below the rose.

Now slice up to your stop cuts, lowering and shaping the leaf. You want the leaf to be approximately half the thickness of the flower, so we have lots of room to give interesting shape to the rose petals. You can see how the paper pattern is carved off as each step is completed.

Continue rounding and shaping until the first leaf has a pleasing appearance. Be sure to give your leaf an interesting shape, not just flat. You could have it curl down to the tip, add a fold, etc. Check out some real roses for ideas. Remember that the shape can always be changed a little bit later, if needed or desired.

Now do the second leaf, using the same process as the first. Notice that there is a slightly different curve on the first. This adds to interest and is closer to reality. No two leaves are alike.

The third leaf is done in the same manner. We are ready to move on to the first petal.

Stop cut the petal first, then start to lower the petal under the ones closest to it by using an angle slice towards your stop cut. (I'm beginning with one of the back petals.) Note that I start with the outside petals, because the formation of the inner ones depend on where the outermost petals begin and end.

Continue angling and shaping until you complete the petal, as shown here. It should be deep at the middle where the petals meet, higher and shaped on the edge.

Let's do the petal on the opposite side to the one we just did. Stop cut it first, then start to lower it from the big petal in front. To give this petal more shape, I've taken off a large triangular piece at the top of the petal, suggesting that this petal curls behind the other petals.

Now you can use your U-gouge to help dig out the central area, giving the petal a more rounded and interesting look.

Continue rounding until you achieve the effect that you like. Don't be afraid to take a little off the edge to get a bit of curl, if you like. Make sure that it is smooth and even, just like a real rose petal.

The next petal will be on the left, just above the first petal. Stop cut and start digging into this cut along the side next to the petal on the right. This should be rather deep towards the middle part of the petal. We will give a more rounded edge to the outer side. As you continue along, don't forget that this petal should also be tucked under the large petal at the very bottom and the large petal at the top.

Finish rounding and shaping this petal. Don't worry, you can always go back and make adjustments later.

Now we will work on the large petal at the top of the rose. It will be higher than the two petals on either side of it, but tucked well under the center of the rose. As usual, start with a stop cut, then deepen the area closest to the center of the flower.

To add interest to this petal, I am putting a scooped cut along the edge to achieve a curled appearance. Note that the scoop is irregular, thus making it more realistic.

Here is what you are aiming for.

We need to create the impression of depth at the center (trumpet) portion of the flower. The side that I have colored in with pencil will be done first and the area colored in red will be the counterpart on the opposite side. To start, make a stop cut where the penciled area meets the petal just above it.

We need to remove some wood on the side so that we will have lots of room to make it look well rounded. I'm pointing with my knife to the area that I removed. Notice how deep it is.

Now round and taper this section underneath the large petal at the bottom.

Follow the same steps for the red section on the other side. Depending on how this red section turns out, the little area above it (colored in yellow in the next photo) may become part of the petal next to it (green in the next photo) or drop down and become part of the big petal at the back. Each time I make the rose, it turns out a little differently.

To show you know how things can change, here's a completed rose in which the red section took over and became the complete trumpet, while the yellow section became part of the large petal at the back. This came about as a result of shaping the middle. Both started out much the same.

This area has now been completed. Note that I have also gone ahead and carved the large central petal below it, although I will discuss the steps for that later. I carved it now in order to best show you the relationship of all the petals.

Stop cut and begin shaping the next petal on the left. Remember, you only see the top edge, not the whole petal.

Continue shaping and rounding. This petal should have the appearance of going behind the remaining paper portion.

Next we will carve the corresponding petal on the opposite side. This one is more of a rolled back petal than the full one. Make sure you get a nice deep cut on the edge towards the middle.

We need to be sure there is enough distinction on the other side of that rolled back edge, so it's a good idea to stop cut and slice down a little bit more to guarantee enough room to curl it.

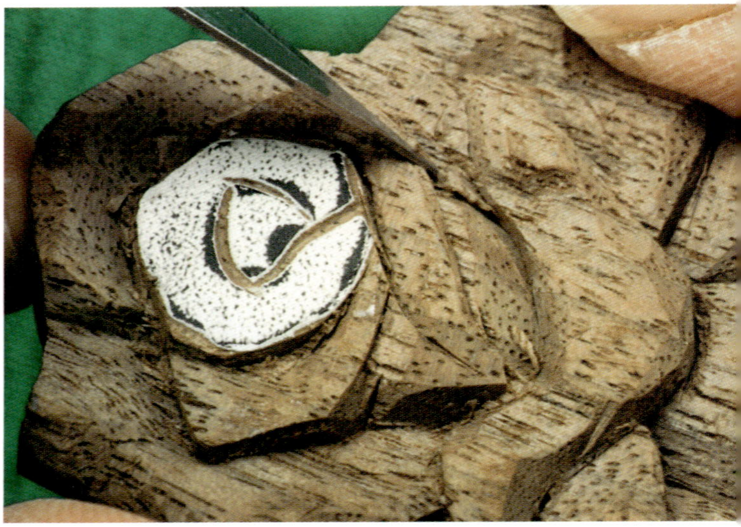

Go ahead and shape this petal by rounding and lowering the outside edge. This will make it appear as if it is curled back. If you need to, increase the angle on the other side; you can even undercut the edge area if needed or desired.

Before we go any further, our trumpet needs some adjustment. The thickness at the very bottom of this petal needs to be adjusted to give the appearance of a finer, thinner edge, going down towards the center – wider at the top, thinner at the middle. We also need to make sure the other side of the trumpet is tucked under this folded petal.

Here's what the adjusted section looks like.

Now let's go back and carve that big central petal. Frequently, it ends up being carved somewhere in the middle, rather than at this point. In fact, it's often helpful (as noted above) to do it as we are working on the trumpet area to be sure everything lines up properly. The exact progression or order as you carve your flower is not carved in stone, so if you work in a different order, that's OK. First I do a scooping cut to start laying this petal down and back towards the leaves. This cut needs to be quite deep where it joins the trumpet, since the trumpet is inside of this petal.

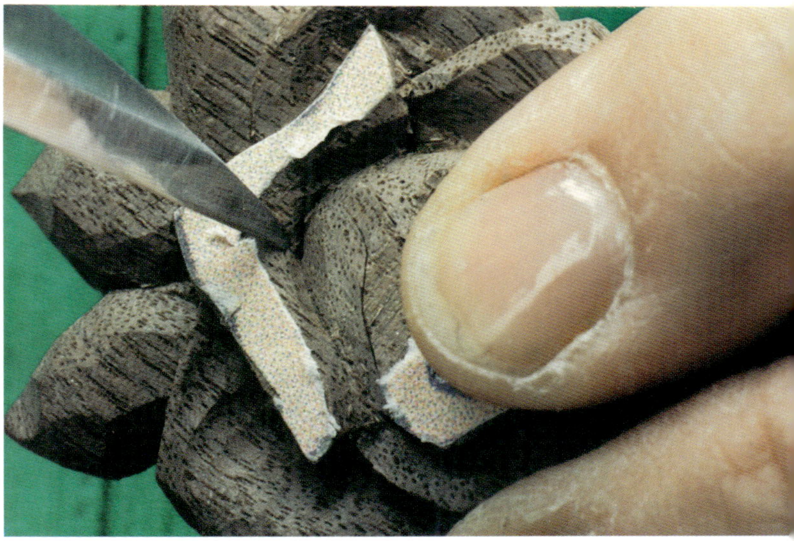

This is how deep you should be aiming for.

Now start rounding the lower edge of this petal. Add variety as you go.

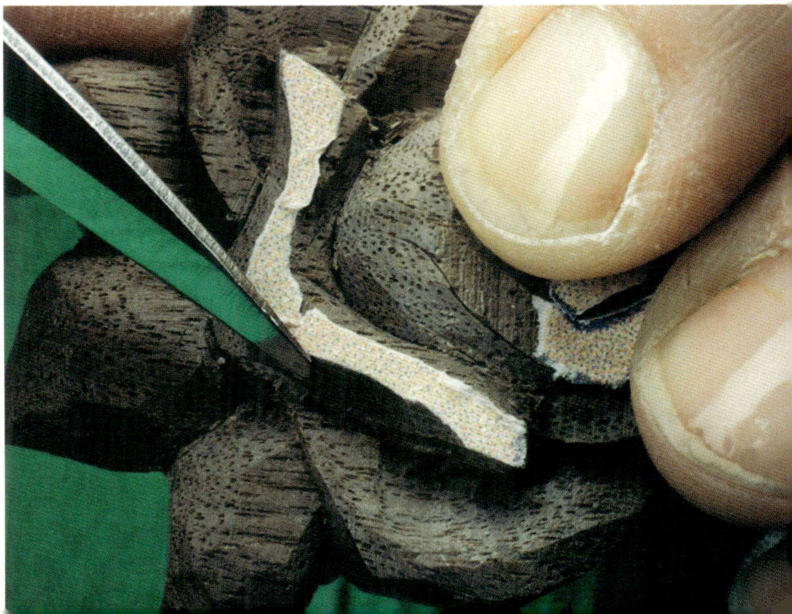

To help round the flower, tip the ends slightly in the direction of the red arrows. You don't need to do a lot here, just enough to give the appearance or suggestion of a rounded surface.

Here you can see how the ends are tapered towards the edges. I've now marked two areas in green where I will make a little indentation. These will become the lowest parts of the flower on either side. If you have difficulty with this, try using a U-gouge. Now continue on and finish up the petal so that it is smooth and flowing.

The flower to this point.

Let's finish the innermost parts of the rose. The yellow section can be made into one continuous petal or you can break it down into more than one part. Sometimes the actual grain may force you into one of these options.

First we need to establish that the yellow section is on the outside of the red one. To do this, make a deeper trough between the two to begin the shaping, tipping the yellow petal under the red. Use a U-gouge to help you as necessary. The left side illustrates the beginning stages of tucking the yellow under the red; the right side illustrates how I've extended that tuck out towards the edges of my flower. You may need to lower the petal just below to make sure this petal is higher than it. Continue along, smoothing out the yellow part. The edges of the yellow are slightly rounded, but should not be completely circular. You can also start working on the red part, which will be going down towards the trumpet – as the inside of a flower would do in real life. If you can fit in an indentation or two, this adds a lot of interest. This is a very small area to work in, so don't worry if it's not perfect.

In this picture, the yellow petal is pretty much completed. The red one is shaped, but we need to add a couple of fine lines to suggest the curled (waiting to be unfurled) nature of the flower. I've used a pencil to draw in some lines on what was the red area where we will add some fine detail, and also drawn lines on the leaves where we will add a center line.

Finish by coating with a water based acrylic varnish. Multiple coats are best, and don't forget the back side!

Adding details. I often make a little V notch with my V-tool, then bring a line down to make an interesting middle. Play around and have some fun. I usually spend lots of time getting my rose just the way I want it. I may even undercut in places (that is, cut away the area underneath to increase the shadow and make the petal look like it's standing out more). Don't rush! I generally don't worry about how tidy the flower is until this point in case I need to change something due to a chip, funny grain, etc.

Here are two examples of the completed rose pin. Both started from the same blank, but due to differences in the grain (or the carver's mood at the time) they look somewhat different. Both are pleasing. Of the hundreds of these I've carved, there are no two that look exactly alike. Add your pinback or magnet and you are done!

Gallery

Example of a rose stamp that I had made by an office supply store, along with the resulting pin.

A stamped blank with its finished counterpart.

Two different commercially made rose stamps.

A beaver pin that I purchased, along with the start of my version of the same pin.

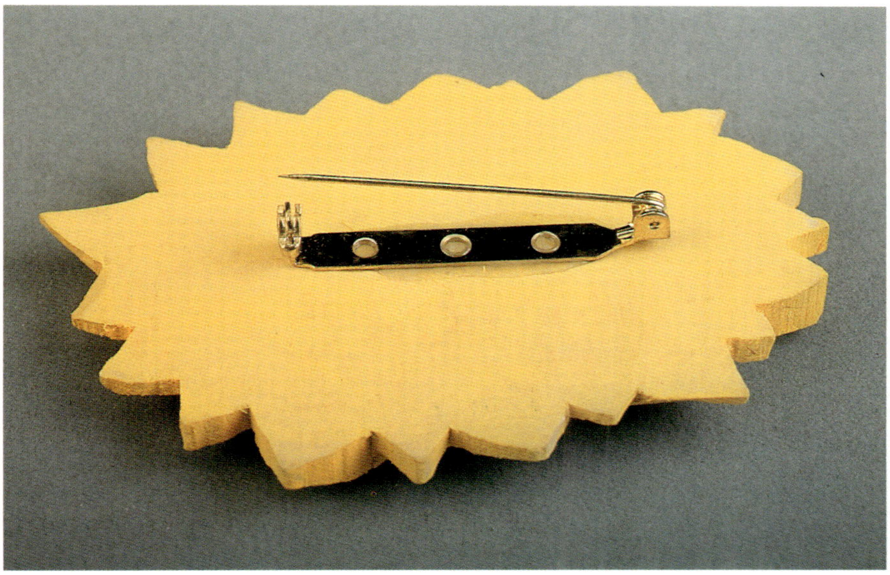

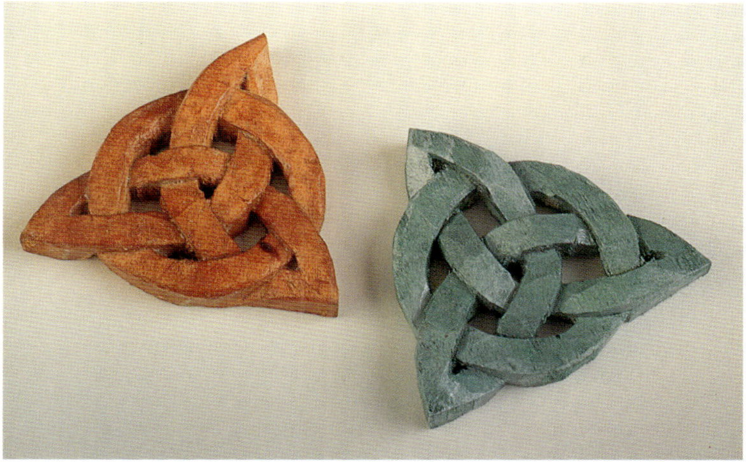

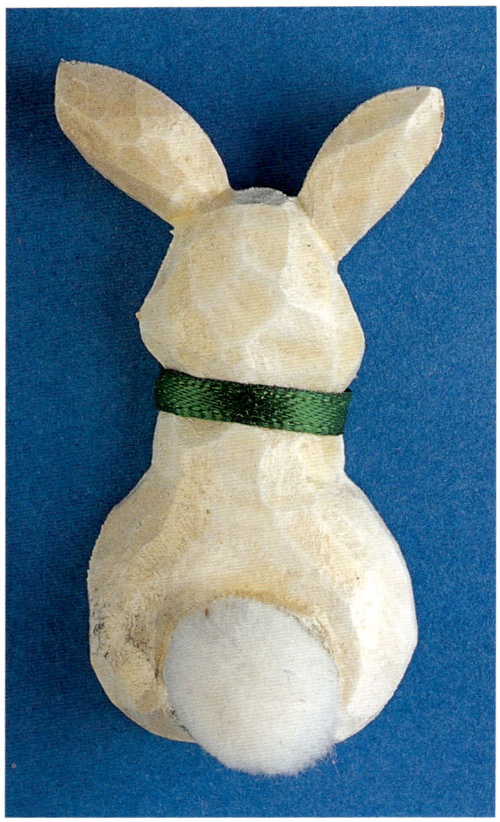